Contents

GH00455333

The Shift

The starry sky, her apex roof,

Her comfort, light of moon,

She walks about her concrete bed,

In heels that break too soon,

She lurks and shakes in shadows dark,

No friend to help her out,

She's virgin, on the lowest low,

No powder for her snout,

A car pulls up, the window down,

He calls her to the curb,

His eyes near pop, his tongue so wet,

He thinks she looks superb,

He drives so fast into the trees,

To have his horrid way,

She peels the stockings from her legs,

And chokes him til he's grey,

Back on her patch, a week anew,

Beneath her moonlit sky,

The teenage girl pulls up her stocks,

A twinkle in her eye.

The Little Boy Who Longed For Love

Full of a might, determined roar,

A passion sharp enough to floor,

Still, easy tasks were difficult for,

The little boy who longed for love,

He'd laugh and play the childish way,

The brightest smile on display,

'I'm doing fine' is what he'd say,

The little boy who longed for love,

He needs not now the lying skill,

He tells the truth, his life's a thrill,

Although deep somewhere I am still,

That little boy who longed for love.

Be Like Elephant

Like elephant. Who roam so free,

And tread the dust so gracefully,

The patient, silent, gentle kind,

Leave visons captured in the mind,

It's they who show us love is key,

The message hidden, some don't see,

What lies behind this giant's plea,

We can't fall down, we'd be resigned,

Like elephant.

So go for which in you believe,

And strive to conquer land and sea,

You never know what you might find,

Today your stars may have aligned,

Remember just to always be,

Like elephant.

She Waits For Me

She waits for me, though I can't come,

My trains delayed, her hearts a drum,

I need to wipe the tears that spill,

Present her one last daffodil,

Oh, how for her, my love does thrum,

She's silent, circling thumb and thumb,

Wondering of me, what's become,

The rain is thrashing down but still,

She waits for me,

Across the track, I'm nearly numb,

With raw emotion, overcome,

She's beauty of the highest bill,

I'm smiling, climbing heaven's hill,

But while my corpse still lies in slum,

She waits for me.

Money

Sometimes I watch the seconds slowly pass,

And still believe I'm running out of time,

Bound by the greed society does class,

Important such, that we must spend our prime,

Both doing something we refuse to love,

And giving up the dreams we long to dare,

In search of something paper which has drove,

Some countries and some people not to share,

Of course, we cannot rid it from our lives,

But surely there's a better way to live,

For, if true love could be the thing that thrives,

We'd surely then learn somehow to forgive,

Until we plant this small harmonic seed,

Our lives will be forever ruled by greed.

The Snap

The client came in clumsiness,

She thought the guy a fool,

The camera pan though, changed the man,

Who sat upon her stool,

Eyes as dark as raven's wings,

Fresh blood splashed on his lip,

This cocky snide, so full of pride,

She nearly lost her grip,

A stink then struck her nostrils, see,

The smell she smelled was death,

Her camera snapped and quick she flapped,

Outside to catch her breath,

She calmly called back through the room,

'Ok, we'll do one more',

He made no sound, that's when she found,

The puddle on the floor,

A fear did prickle up her spine,

It played on every nerve,

The door was shut, the lights were cut,

The darkness stole her verve,

She pawed around, 'Get out! Get out!',

Then goose-bumped flesh met knife,

The camera caught, the wire taut,

That took the snapper's life

Ali Terration and the Journey

The train begins to pull away,

I sit and shake in fear,

I'm scared to let you down my love,

Let's slow things down my dear,

She swirls at me seductively,

Star of my teenage nights,

She tickles, touches, tortures me,

And dances in delight,

The train slows down, my stop but one,

I'm feeling most unripe,

I go to go but then think no,

I've never met her type,

She leaves me then, for five or ten,

And I feel fine here on,

But then I glance and gape in fear,

Because I see she's gone,

'Come back' I plea, 'can't you see',

I'm scared that I won't strive,

Let's go too far in your old car,

Please take me for a ride,

The train it halts and then I bolt,

Delirious, to say,

That I was blue, and she was who,

Took this Prince all the way.

A Longing For Love

I long to lay beneath the stars,

And walk by rivers too,

I crave the touch of female hands,

But only yours will do,

I yearn to see you bite that lip,

With pleasure in your eyes,

A passion etched across your face,

Where love can't find disguise,

I long to taste you, beautiful,

Then lick my dripping lips,

I long to let my fingers roam,

And watch you rock those hips,

I need to nose your scent again,

Your smell, most always, sweet,

Please say you'll stay just one more day,

Or I shall feel defeat,

I wish to hear you whisper wants,

The dreams you crave the most,

And if the morn should interrupt,

I'll bring you up your toast,

The Smiler

They say, 'he lives nearby your street',

'The darkest man you'll ever meet',

'His house, abandoned, windows blown',

'The nearby swings, swing on their own',

Are these just stories people say?,

You swear you've seen the shadows sway,

For here they tell, 'he likes to hide',

'And snatch young children from the slide',

'His eyes are peace, they'll draw you in',

'But then you'll see that horror grin',

'Those joyful lips with crimson stain',

'And sharp white pearls which pierce the vein',

Back home, at night, your mind, still blue,

You find this smiler's eating you,

Is Jacky safe? Are you quite sure?,

Just quickly knock his bedroom door,

When there's no answer, in you tread,

Your body shaking, filled with dread,

You calmly slide the duvet back,

To find the mangled corpse of Jack.

The Child's Laughter

The soft suns melting, stealing light,

But we won't budge, bring on the night!

For here I heard it sweet but slight,

The sound of a child's laughter,

'Daddy listen I've got a joke',

Laughter spilled through the words he spoke,

I led and longed when I awoke,

The sound of the child's laughter,

I wait the day when I am shown,

The baby I can call my own,

The only sound our home will know,

The sound of my child's laughter,

The greatest thing the world can teach,

While at the zoo, the park, the beach,

Amongst the yell, the cry, the screech,

The sound of a child's laughter.

Norma

While freezing metal tore my wrists up,

Digging, searching for the bone,

Through teary eyes I traced the water,

Thinking of my lovely home,

She, so crazy, like the river,

Standing, snow-white, grinning glee,

Left hand clutching closed, her jacket,

Right hand firmly gripping me,

Her eyes alone, a crazy circus,

Chilling me unto my core,

'You won't be leaving til you admit,

That you've slept with me before'

Give In

Oh! Let me love thy loving heart,

The beats I fell for from the start,

The organ mine cannot now part,

Oh! Why won't you give in,

Oh let me play that golden flesh,

That sways beneath thy tightened dress,

Such mys'try keeps my thinking fresh,

Oh! Why don't you give in,

I watch you love the wand'ring eyes,

And play the part of girl's surprise,

A flirting lust, beneath it lies,

Now give it up, give in,

Completely bare yourself to me,

Your heart, your soul and sexually,

Dare, let me go beyond my dreams,

And show me you'll give in.

The Walk

My coat was zipped against the blow,

The coldest wind I'll ever know,

I left my footprints in the snow,

For her to see,

Why won't these thoughts that hurt me so,

Just let me be,

I struggled forward through the night,

With only trees to shield the light,

They swung and swept, begged me to fight,

But on I pressed,

My mind was plagued with horrid mites,

Which gave no rest,

Two men approached in horse and cart,

I said good evening with my heart,

They frowned and scoffed and laughed in part,

At me, one spat,

The stone I threw before I dart,

Knocked off his hat,

I found the tree that looked of use,

One leafless, tall and quite recluse,

I fashioned slowly then the noose,

Began to climb,

My tired eyes closed on abuse,

Come had my time.

You'll Find Him

You'll find him bathed in orange light,

You'll find him on the bench,

On unforgiving wood, he seeks,

A thirst he can't quite quench,

For one hot day in June, July,

A solemn tear did fall,

The cab door slammed and whisked her off,

Toward a man named Paul,

He begged and begged her not to leave,

He pulled upon her dress,

His heart was ripped and pecked to bits,

The man became a mess,

It's five years now bang on the day,

And still he sits with yearn,

Both silently and hoping she,

Will to him once return,

You'll find him bathed in orange light,

You'll find him on the bench,

On unforgiving wood, he seeks,

A thirst he can't quite quench.

Please and Thankyou

These thoughts please take away from me,

I try to cope, but still they feeze,

Oh, can't you somehow set them free,

So they don't bug,

They're like a cancer or disease,

My heart they tug,

Oh! Please forgive me this mistake,

I drove right in the lover's lake,

And now my loving heart does ache,

From time to time,

I beg of you, a boost create,

This wall, I'd climb,

Oh! Why does man resemble leech?

Or panting dog, always on heat,

And try to tempt your love to cheat,

Under your snoot,

I guess like Ad' they're temp'd to eat,

Forbidden fruit,

Still, lastly thanks for all you've done,

Like mould the man I have become,

I'm stronger now, I'll overcome,

Life's horrid hoard,

I'll never doubt you, rain or sun,

So thankyou Lord.

The Ballad Of Case: 1275

Admitted in the seventeenth,

His brain just half alive,

Restrained by hefty, fearsome men,

Case one two seven five,

His bad eye faced the solid wall,

His good eye stared you down,

But still he'd sit until she sat,

The nurse in knee length gown,

He'd slide on over, listen close,

He'd do just what she said,

He liked the way that nursey spoke,

They way she rubbed his head,

Then one hot day, a new nurse came,

Her neck damp, with a sweat,

He forced his hands upon it tight,

Not once feeling regret,

Near perfectly, her nurse clothes fit,

The pants, although, did peeve,

For then, case one two seven five,

Made off on that warm eve.

The Beautiful

Flowers bloom colourf'ly,

Red, Orange, Tan,

Words become poetry,

Boy becomes man,

Owls swoop gracefully,

Feathered wings spread,

Leaves finding coloured shape,

Tan, Orange, Red,

Mists dance round mountain tops,

Roads barely drove,

Setting suns like beetroot,

Turning sky's mauve,

A foals first footsteps as,

They tred the mud,

A smile on my lady's face,

Her heart full of love.

The Life of the Party

A strange, outrageous, funky suit,

A bulbous, blood-red nose,

A grin spread wide, from cheek to cheek,

But wait, his mouth is closed,

His hands are gloved in snow-black silk,

They help perform his trick,

Illusion, animal of balloon,

This rabbit's coat is thick,

From place to place, his cake-white face,

Is known for being kind,

But oh the shock, if they'd just clock,

What's really on his mind,

He'd really bloom in any room,

This entertainer's smart,

You'd never twig, his cold, blue wig,

Does parallel his heart.

Sonnet 2 (My Love For You)

So dammed by the perils of the boyfriend,

But snaking shallow slowly building blue,

Seeking out your estuary of heart-mend,

My love's a river flowing just for you,

My paper-boated thoughts, float, meander,

A glance of you's enough to burst its bank,

Your smile sweetly welcomed this outlander,

I dream the day the dam is but a plank,

You, to me, are like the sun, you're shining,

I picture you to fill the valleys void,

Companionship's what my heart is pining,

The weight of loneliness is asteroid,

So long as flowers helped by sunshine, grow,

The river of my love for you will flow.

Crowned in Victory

Crowned in victory,

A muse for my poetry,

Enveloped in beauty,

A new kind of love,

Sweet, calming, flowery,

Like a flavoured potpourri,

Tectonic chemistry,

More every meet,

Left with imagery,

A prospect so lovely,

A substantial hope that these,

Stars do align.

The Mask

Tonight lay peaceful, calm and still,

But for mother bird's call,

Tall trees looked ill and bore the chill,

That swept the infant's school,

Thin hallways dusty, silent, dank,

The sound of footsteps none,

The putrid rank of rotting, stank,

The classrooms out but one,

This noon, the mask, had had her caught,

The shears began their play,

Her rooms for teachings, lessons taught,

Was paint in bloody spray,

Then Mask became the winds that blew,

Around the dusking town,

The moon peered through the clouds that grew,

The rain was lashing down.

Griselda Dove

When Thee awoke by swishing calm,

And felt a sand upon the palm,

Thee eyed a sky, star-filled but clear,

Before her cry near pierced your ear,

'Excuse me nymph are you alright?'

But nymph on-hurried through the night,

Bare naked but a thin white gown,

Thee followed on towards the town,

Tiresome but filled with gee,

Thee's prayer: her soul will soon be free,

Alas! She's stopped on Boscombe Pier,

She's seeking, searching, someone dear,

'Grisilda Dove! Grisilda Dove,

Can't you see, it's you I love',

Thee watches, wonders, hopelessly,

While this fair ghost floats out to sea.

The Lost One

Soft tears, my one last gift to you,

For now we cannot meet,

I learned your death, my life was wrecked,

Just mem'ries, my receipt,

My darkest nights, you lit like stars,

On countless times, it's true,

The way you'd perfect practiced skill,

Yet always found the new,

Still, inspiration doesn't cut,

The word is far too mere,

See, you have touched my soul and now,

Hearts don't break around here,

You'll always be so dear to me,

Yes gone but not forgot,

No day goes by without a thought,

For love won't let me stop.

The Proposal

The diesel locomotive chuffed on late,

Their gorgeous destination nearing still,

The nerves of he were dancing while they wait,

To glimpse the ruined castle on the hill,

When finally, the crumbling stairs were climbed,

And green'ry views of beauty calmed the sting,

He found for them, an empty room, to hide,

Then fell and gifted her a diamond ring,

'Take this a sign of my eternal love,

Then cherish it as I will cherish you,

I'll boast you to the world and it's above,

Until I'm in the ground both cold and blue',

The worries that she had did then unfurl,

For now, she truly knew she was his girl.

Paradise

Where forest fields, all year, entice,

Where hawk and falcon glide for mice,

The shortest visit does suffice,

And take our fear,

This truly was a paradise,

When we were here,

We sat beneath the orange tree,

You whispered to me lovingly,

I took my hand from off your knee,

And wiped a tear,

In perfect time for you to see,

The baby deer,

Your lips lit up, your face was gripped,

Our thoughts escaped, my heart was fixed,

But oh! Then how your health was flipped,

Within the year,

Our time together torn and clipped,

My life, unclear,

But now I sit despite the pain,

Beneath our tree, beneath the stain,

Your mem'ry always in my brain,

And atmosphere,

At least for ever and a day,

Ill hold you near,

The forest fields do still entice,

Still, hawk and falcon glide for mice,

But visits short do not suffice,

I miss you dear,

The place we once called paradise,

Now insincere.

21766500R00016

Printed in Poland
by Amazon Fulfillment
Poland Sp. z o.o., Wrocław